Winner of the L. E. Phillabaum Poetry award for 2013

poems
poems

Civil Wars

poems

DAVID R. SLAVITT

 *Louisiana State University Press Baton Rouge*

Published by Louisiana State University Press

Manufactured in the United States of America

Designer: Barbara Neely Bourgoyne
Typefaces: Univers, display; Ingeborg, text

Library of Congress Cataloging-in-Publication Data
Slavitt, David R., 1935–

[Poems. Selections]
Civil Wars : poems / David R. Slavitt. — LSU Paperback edition.
pages cm
ISBN 978-0-8071-5180-8 (paper : alk. paper) — ISBN 978-0-8071-5181-5 (pdf) —
ISBN 978-0-8071-5182-2 (epub) — ISBN 978-0-8071-5183-9 (mobi)
I. Title.
PS3569.L3C58 2014
811'.54—dc23

2012048400

The paper in this book meets the guidelines for permanence and durability of the Committee on Production Guidelines for Book Longevity of the Council on Library Resources. ♾

Some of these poems have appeared in *Boulevard, The Hopkins Review, The New Criterion, The New England Review, Light, Pequod,* and *Per Contra.* The translation of Pierre de Fermat's "Give Way to God, or the Dying Christ" was first published by Springer Science + Business Media B.V. in *The Mathematical Intelligencer* 34, no. 2 (2012): 3–5.The translation from Old English of "The Battle of Maldon" was published in *The Word Exchange,* W. W. Norton & Co., 2011.

for Janet

CONTENTS

part one

Poems

part two

Renditions

Civil Wars

part one

Poems

Isaac

After that grotesque business up on the mountain,
Abraham comes down and goes to Beersheba,
but what about Isaac?
                                        No, not a word about him.

A mistake?
                    There cannot be mistakes in the Torah!
The hole is there to let the rabbis fill it,
to see through that emptiness the light of truth.

In study houses, then, those earnest old men
told one another stories, made up midrashim
to answer the question that loomed. Maybe he went
out into the desert? Maybe out there he met
Ishmael, and the half brothers compared
their sad stories. And maybe reconciled?
Or at least came to that delicate equipoise
of civility relatives need to be together.

Another rabbi says that it's too much,
that there's no need and therefore no warrant to go
quite that far into the desert shimmer.
Be sensible. Think! Where could he have gone?
We need an answer. What would a young man do?
Say he spends a year or maybe more
at some yeshiva!
                                    Where would there be a yeshiva?
Torah is eternal: although it had not
yet been written, it had always been written.
Its sacred fire always burned, like the bush
God allowed Moses to see that does not
consume itself and therefore burns even now.

So if there was Torah, there were yeshivas,
high in the sky, or perhaps just around the corner,
though not yet visible. Maybe he studied there.

But who, then, could his teachers have been?
Us!
And what would we have been doing until that moment?
Waiting for Isaac, of course.
As we are still waiting.

Tisiphone

Nobody sees her but me, but I do, often,
often enough not to react anymore,
not that I care what other T riders think,
or other shoppers. It's her I worry about,
the horrid grey figure that disappears
at the end of the aisle, say, at the Triscuit display
or on the street, getting off a bus as I
get on another. She is, in that old sense,
a familiar, following me. She isn't stalking
so much as presiding, naked, with whips in her hand,
the meager, pendulous dugs, the piercing glare
transfixing me, as if Juno had sent her
or, better, it's all on her own, in her spare time.
I worried about her at first. For a long time
she made me uneasy. Furies often do that,
but after a while she was company of a kind,
even reassuring. (Oddly enough
I think she wears patchouli.)
                                                  I know who I am:
the one to whom she pays attention, the one
who's able to see her. Terror? We all have that.
But who has such visitations? For whom else
does she lurk in the dairy section of Star Market?
Pride? In her? For that sin she may spare me
(but I have plenty of others she knows about).
My nightmares are mine. It's these daytime apparitions
that give my torments stature, even importance.
One day she will point her bony finger
at me, and speak my name and brandish her whip,
but it will be an exchange between old friends,
and who can say, after these encounters,
what further metamorphoses may ensue?

Intimate:

To imply, to suggest in a subtle manner, to hint,
but not in a coy or teasing way, to assume
that those to whom you speak will understand,
having so long understood so much. You need not
blurt it bluntly, if you are not so disposed,
but may indicate, with the slightest gesture, a mere

change in your tone of voice, and they not only
know but understand deeply what you say
without saying, or try to say but can't.
These are intimates; this is intimacy.
That long *a* at the end, as you see, shifts
ever so slightly, relaxes, becomes a short *i*

or a mere schwa, and this at once transforms
the verb into another part of speech,
an adjective or even perhaps a noun,
meaning those close friends to whom you need not
go to any great lengths to make yourself clear,
because they have already come more than halfway.

Tortoise

You pull in your head and legs and tuck in your tail
to shut out the affronts and thoughtless assaults
as if they were from some other world, to withdraw
to that sweet dark and the reassuring rhythm

of your beating heart that cannot be broken again
by ex-wife, children, disappointing grandchildren,
as you endure, like a rock, inert, indifferent,
invulnerable . . . that's what we tortoises learned

over the millions of years, with each of us living
not merely decades but hundreds of years to add
his tiny hard-won grain of strategic wisdom
to the species' collective hoard. Inward, inward,

and let them say what they want, or not say, not even
talk, or acknowledge you are there at the table.
The tender flesh that used to feel such wounds
is hidden within the elegant shell they may use

after you're dead for combs or spectacle frames.
But you won't feel it, any more then than now,
and sooner or later, one way or another,
if the noise stops, you can stick your head out again.

Dancing Bear

Barefoot on the hot beach sand, you try
not to step too heavily: in pain
you hop, shifting your weight. An innocent eye
might suppose you were dancing to some strain

that only you could hear. And this is the way
the Russians teach bears to dance, heating the floor:
the animals are forced to hop so they
can minimize the pain. Pity the poor

cubs of course, but also their trainer who
is playing the concertina near the bears.
Pavlov's trick with his dogs was related to
this practice: the concertina scares

the animals always into a gait that can pass
for dancing and even joy. And crowds approve.
The trainer probably loves his bears but he has
a hot floor under him too that makes him move

in the ways he does. He cannot disobey
Fate, who may affect a high silk hat
and cutaway coat—but these do not convey
cheerfulness. He and his bears know that.

Hour Glass

Above the cincture (or is it a sphincter?) the narrow now of the enormous
glass, the future bleeds from what remains of the reservoir.
Like sundials on cloudy days or after dark, these devices
are useless unless we look up or down. What
we see is the steady stream of
g
r
a
n
u
l
e
s
on the way down.
Not sand, which would be neutral and easy,
but all the pills, the tablets, caplets and capsules,
that measure out our days. The runoff below, whatever its size,
is irrelevant. Our worry is above: even if we could who would dare look?

Comb

Sure, poems are momentary stays
against confusion, but so is the comb I use
every morning, imposing or, say, teasing
out of the white tangle the illusion
of civility and order to which we all
aspire. Even better, if the comb
had longer teeth and could get under the skull
to rake those whorls of the brain to a Zen garden

of pattered white pebbles that might last.
Apparently Frost never combed his hair,
having learned to limit his expectations,
as I have done myself. Still, seeing that
tousled apparition staring back
every morning, I comb it once again.

Civil Wars

The Civil War, as Thomas Hobbes maintained,
resulted from the sudden explosion of print
in which semieducated revolutionarics
misunderstood their Tacitus and Livy.
Reading without proper guidance, he said,
would transform England into one of those ignorant
kingdoms of darkness.
The Church had always known this
and kept the Bible from common dirty hands
lest reception theory produce a thousand,
a million different impromptu religions. Writing
is mostly misunderstood. Without the *drash,*
the *pshat* is a snare, inviting absurd opinions
and encouraging Protestantism that moves its lips
as it reads a sacred or even a secular text.
The *yad's* finger bounces from word to word,
but what God whispered into Moses' ear
is an indispensable part of the whole truth.

The plainest text can be tricky for the naïf,
as God surely intended.
DRINK COCA COLA
means what it says, no? What else could it mean?
But then we parse it. What else, after all,
would anyone do with Coke? It can be a douche,
as people in trailer parks and cheap motels
all over the world have learned. What the words
say is that you can *also* drink it (but not
from the same bottle). Put stress on the first word
and that's where you are. The *drash's* touch has turned
a simple imperative into a subtle reminder
of what it doesn't say. Mere words will shimmer,
will sport like flying fish in a sea of meanings.

Or change the figure and think of the mad misprisions
in which writers conceal ourselves. The ink
of the squid was never meant to elucidate:
the point is to blacken the otherwise clear water.

Spy

It isn't the bugs, the meets, the risky uploads,
or the rare bag-jobs that wear you down, but the rest,
the appearance of living normally in a flat
that is almost entirely fictive, even eating
notional meals. Nothing you do is real—
or nothing that anyone knows about. Each moment
is thought out ahead of time and calculated
to be without interest, studiedly ordinary.
Alone, as not even hermits could imagine,
you pretend, and pretend not to pretend. It's fatiguing,
corrodes the spirit, a burden you never quite
learn to carry lightly. You lie down at night
to dream an impostor's nightmares that you share
with the other agents, none of whom you know.

Tinnitus

It is there all the time.

It may be, but when I'm asleep, I can't hear it. So it is only there if I am conscious. It is, then, the sound of being conscious.

A high hiss, the kind of noise a steam radiator used to make. It is the sound my brain perceives, and the brain believes in itself—as how can it not? It is the sound of my brain.

A steam-operated brain? Why not? But it could as easily be a sound that the body makes—of blood passing through the tiny vessels. It is not unlike the sound of water running constantly in the next room.

There is a pulse to it, which is my pulse in the artery near the eardrum. No change in pitch, but, if I pay careful attention, I can perceive a periodic increase in volume, which is annoying or soothing, depending on my mood. One should be grateful to have his heart working and blood flowing.

There are cures but they are experimental and involve, some of them, shock therapy. Life is shock therapy enough. Better than such drastic measures, I could simply persuade myself that this is a good thing. After a while, the tinnitus can seem to be the noise that time makes. There is no time except the interval between events, which requires consciousness to notice.

So this development is both a closing down and an opening up. Both an impoverishment and an enrichment. It comes with age, as debility does. And as wisdom does—or at least the wisdom to understand a simple sentence: *I set before you this day a blessing and a curse.*

The curses we can deal with: blessings weigh us down.

Il Trovatore: The Villanelle

The Gypsy threw the baby in the fire.
Bad things are likely to happen now:
evil, nobility, and mischance conspire.

There will be savage hatred and desire
seething in the boiling pot somehow.
The Gypsy threw the baby in the fire.

The flames of those mixed passions flicker higher
than reason, which is absent, might allow;
evil, nobility, and mischance conspire.

We listen to the singers whom we admire
performing in a tale we'd disavow:
of the Gypsy and the baby in the fire.

But hammering on their anvils, the male choir
figures the fate to which all men must bow.
The Gypsy threw the baby in the fire:
evil, nobility, and mischance conspire.

Sirens

There were three of them or, some authors say, two
with bodies of women or else of feathered birds
with women's heads, or sometimes potters had them

with bearded faces. One of the versions supposes
that if their fatally beautiful singing failed—
as of course it did when Odysseus passed by, bound

as he was to the mast with the oarsmen's ears all stopped
with beeswax to make them immune—the sirens would perish.
A hard rule, but what else can happen to magic

after it has been reduced to a mere
performance in recital and concert halls?
"Breathtaking," we say, but we still breathe.

So artists should die? But, then, alas, they will,
every one of them, however gifted. They try
(practice, practice) and come close to divine

perfection, but we applaud and then go home.
For writers it's less dramatic, but we, too, do
our best and, although we do not admit it, dream

that the words will live on, that our hold on someone's attention
here or there, may continue at random, blips
frequent enough to become a steady low tone,

not quite the song the sirens sang, but close.

Ptolemaic Astronomy

> *The body was taken to move on a small circle, the epicycle, the center of which itself moved on a circle, the deferent, around the center of the world. In most cases the deferent was an eccentric circle like that of the sun. In the case of the moon, the eccentric deferent itself constituted a large epicycle turning on a smaller deferent centered on the earth. From a starting position of conjunction with the sun, the center of the deferent revolved from east to west at about 11° a day, the center of the epicycle from west to east at about 13° a day (with respect to the earth), and the moon on the epicycle in the same direction as the deferent at about 24° a day.*

You learn all that and you're not going to be too eager
to let it go. Never mind how the world
has to be, for theological reasons,
the middle of everything, this is what you took
years to master. And now that heretic Polack
has shown it all up?
Even supposing he's right,
who will believe it? Your mind follows your gut
and you know that you must be the center, the others
whirling around in circles and epicycles
that stars and planets maybe imitate.
"I" is the unwobbling pivot, the pole,
and any other giddy idea affronts
what we discovered when we first learned to stand.

The Copernicans are right. We are forced
to give lip service to this. Otherwise no
diploma, no job, no hope, and the fugitive life
of Lollards, their eyes peeled, and meeting in secret.
I dare not admit what I think, even to friends
who will turn me in, or, almost as bad, just laugh.

String theory posits thirteen dimensions. Why not?
If you keep a cat, you have a whole new set of dimensions
along with those you live in.
The ancient system
had a center, which was, of course, where you were.
Claudius Ptolemy, who figured it out, was named that
having been born in Ptolemais Hermii.
His center was an Alexandrian rooftop,
but for each of us it's different, which simplifies things.

☾

And time, too, they have going straight
from then to now to beyond that, like an arrow
that never finds its target. We know better,
can describe its whorls and curious loops, the chance
conjunction of a moment on the knife-edge
with another moment, still burning, alive,
comet-bright, with that same elliptical orbit.
No cataclysm comes, but a subtle prompting,
a hot day and a dusty road with weeds,
sumac, I think, verdant on either side,
and I am seven or eight years old again.
Einstein's curving trolley cars in Zurich
are fearsome, but I think they're a parlor trick,
and where I am, we believe our lying eyes.

☾

You have to admire them all,
those old astronomers whose calculations
were all the more dazzling being wrong.
That they could predict the sunrise was a triumph,
but they did more and better than that. Insane
adjustments and rectifications after a while,
can approximate the world. Look at the dust motes
dance in the shaft of sunlight and analyze them
so that you can say, from moment to moment,
where one speck will go, or how two specks

will appear to dance, even though that's an illusion.
You're looking at chaos, or, rather, getting a glimpse
of the chaos you have always looked at and lived in
but could not recognize or admit to yourself.
That you can get up in the morning, get to work,
get back . . . These are all amazing achievements
given that your basic assumptions are all
arbitrary, conventional, probably wrong.
But you make it up and, by an act of faith,
put your foot where the ground is supposed to be,
and seems to be, even if its atoms
are whirling like that dust in Brownian motion,
as is, indeed, your foot, which could go through
the fragile altogether notional crust,
where you're dancing, walking on eggshells, walking on air.

Epitaph for a Headmaster

Ted
Sizer is dead,
who once said:
"If they're old enough to be having sex, they're too old to be at Andover."
And Fate's wry answer?
Colon cancer.

Dinner Toast

Each crystal luster, bright
in itself, both borrows and lends
light from and to the others.
So it is, also, with friends.

I thank you all* for coming
to mark this turn of my year,
where we are most fully ourselves
in our glittering chandelier.

* Fred and Susan Chappell, Kelly Cherry and Burke Davis III, Richard Dillard, Brendan and Ellen Galvin, George and Susan Garrett, Henry and Mooshe Taylor, and Janet Abrahm.

The Washing of the Bodies

> *The Trojans . . . found it hard to recognize each dead man,*
> *so they washed away the blood that was on them and, weeping warm tears,*
> *hefted their bodies up onto the wagons.*
>
> —ILIAD VII

The temptation is not to look, to let the names
go as the life had gone from each of them.
What difference does it make anymore?
                                                            But you can't.
You have to know. It hurts, but you have to
and you wash away the blood, for them of course,
but for yourself, too, so you know whom you have lost,
and the salt sea water you use begets salt tears.

Heroes, yes, but others, cowards, fools,
a kid you barely remember from school whose face
brings back the kid you were, for a moment alive,
and then, like him, gone again and forgotten.

But do not mourn too long. There is work to do;
the wagons are waiting; the sun will soon go down;
and tomorrow we will return to the shedding of blood
that hides so much that we could not otherwise bear.

Harmonica Rascals

To do well a thing that is not worth doing
requires a psychic poise I envy, or else
crude need I don't, but it works out
to the same thing. I think of the Steel Pier
and a thousand men and women spinning plates
on sticks, performing together, while the band played
(of course) "The Sabre Dance," and my smile is not
entirely one of contempt, for which of God's creatures
could think of such a thing, or, having thought of it,
could be prevailed upon somehow to do it?

I remember Borrah Minevich and the Harmonica Rascals,
harmonica playing being one of those other
things that are not worth doing. A kid's toy,
a cowboy's solace, a dopey instrument
Larry Adler tried to elevate
to respectability—for political reasons
to take that prole mouth organ and claim for it
a refinement it never had or even wanted,
not for its sake but for its tacky glimpse
of the people's paradise he was persuaded
he offered to the snobbish, skeptical world.
Minevich didn't think he was so hot
technically on the harmonica. (The politics
I don't think he bothered to address.)

An immigrant from Kiev, he made a living
up in the Catskills but then, always ambitious
as immigrants are, he hired a dozen boys
whom he taught to play. The Harmonica Rascals
made their debut with the one song they'd learned
and were novel enough to get offered more bookings,
so they had to learn more songs.

Minevich conducted, camping it up
with the silly grace of a Ben Blue ballet
that both denied and asserted the performance.
Johnny Puleo was part of the group, a midget
whose shtick was attacking all the other players
and then getting beaten up. He played
a huge bass harmonica—for laughs,
but then it was all for laughs.
After Minevich died, he had his own career,
with his Harmonica Gang.

Jerry Murad played with the Rascals, too,
then left, and established the Harmonicats,
a name that resonates still, however faintly.
They had one hit, "Peg O' My Heart," which took off
during the 1947 strike
of the musicians' union that didn't believe harmonicas
were legitimate instruments.

They're not, but that's the point.
With enormous effort, they can be made
to make something like music,
and at their best are not too painfully bad.

Rascals, Gang, Cats—I do not claim
that these somehow represent the human condition
but then what would?
It would have to be absurd, even stupid,
but also difficult,
and depend, more than is comfortable, on chance.

Escape

For Nina

What a comfort it is, when I am sad
and it has been raining for many days in my soul,
to think that I could get away from all this,
pack my suitcase, or never mind my suitcase,
and go to the ice-cream parlors of Cochabamba.

The sound of a guitar in the gentle night,
the fragrances of frangipani and bougainvillea,
the cries of parrots, and the laughter of young girls
will congratulate me for the boldness of my dreams
while I sit in an ice-cream parlor in Cochabamba.

With mustachioed grandees and señoritas,
with donkey carts decked with fresh-cut flowers,
with the twinkling stars above, or the bright moon,
and a perfect climate, how can one not be happy,
at ease in an ice-cream parlor in Cochabamba?

April 20

On his birthday they would bring flowers to his grave,
if he had a grave. Instead they have to make do
with that of his parents in Leonding at St. Michael's

under a large fir tree. Alois and Klara,
who were not monsters, every year get flowers
intended for Adolf. The house where he was born

in Braunau is marked with a stone bearing the words
Peace, Freedom, Democracy . . . Government nonsense,
so true believers, some from the old days,

and some younger, sorry they missed the war,
go instead to St. Michael's to leave him his flowers,
which also are inadequate substitutions

for the bouquets of Jewish bones he would prefer.

Normandie

It wasn't loose lips that sank her
but a spark from the acetylene torch
of a welder who somehow supposed that life preservers,
because they were buoyant and waterproof, were also
fireproof. No, not at all, and a pile
burst into flames the workmen on the ship
fought for fifteen minutes until they realized
that they were losing. The fire department came
to pump water through their high-pressure hoses
into the stricken vessel, which fairly quickly
capsized and lay there, a huge black ruin—
more than a thousand feet long.

                                                                  She and I
were both seven. From my parents' black Plymouth
on the West Side Highway I could see the poor thing
lying on her side, an object lesson
that not even great size was any protection
from war and the perils I already knew were lurking.

Spinoza

The Amsterdam rabbis were not altogether wrong.
The *kherem* on Spinoza was justified
by everything they believed. He was, in their city,
not just a nuisance but the major threat they perceived
without understanding why or what he threatened.
In 1656 what gabardined man
could imagine Kant, Hegel, Marx, and Freud,
not to mention Nietzsche? The age of reason,
of vertiginous free fall is dawning there
among a small community of Marranos,
who had no choice but to reject it all
and him with it.
Twenty-some years before,
the Church had been wrong in its wrangle with Galileo,
but, as John Paul II admitted, the earth
does move. The rabbis, less silly, worried
that reason would run amok. Ethics without
God? And destruction not only of what they believed
but belief itself.
Kherem? Give over to God
(often by violence) was what they had fled from in Spain.
If we could be there and we had the nerve, we might
tug on a tallit fringe of one of the panel
and point out the uncomfortable repetition
in Amsterdam but with them the inquisitors now.
It's anyway moot. We can't excommunicate Jews,
the *Nürnberger Gesetze* having determined
that with one Jewish grandparent you were
merely a Mischling but two made you a Jew.
Marked thus with our yellow star, confirmed,
believing or not, condemned, we were welcomed forever.

Osip and Boris

Pasternak told him:
It is not literature; it is not poetry. It is suicide.
Osip Emilievich nevertheless continued to recite his poem
about how Stalin was a mustached cockroach.
(For this, he needed advice?)
                                                            But do cockroaches
have mustaches? You have to know the Chukovsky poem
about the huge mustachioed cockroach the forest fears
until a brave sparrow comes and devours him with a deft peck.
So? Would the crude Georgian have slapped his thigh,
laughing and therefore, at least in part, approving?
What he does is surprising. He picks up the phone and calls,
at two in the morning, to ask Comrade Pasternak
if Mandelstam is any good. A master?
But Mandelstam's colleague and worried pal
gives an equivocal answer. Stalin hangs up.
The advice Boris had offered was incomplete:
Be careful what you write, but that's a given;
be very careful about who reads what you've written;
and learn not to trust too much in friends like me.

Conversation with My Father

Whenever my father bought a new car
he would go into a funk, worried that this one
might be his last.
                                        At last he turned out to be right.
I'm older now than he was when he died
and wish I could explain to him that the converse
is also true.
                              I opened a new bottle
of vitamin pills this morning. Each one contains
365 pills. This could be
my last, but then, as I threw away the empty
I noticed a minuscule feeling of satisfaction
in having got through another one.
                                                            I can see
the look on his face, scornful, also amused,
but most of all indulgent that we were different.

Sestina on Six End-Words of Petrarch

Every dumb beast that lives on the earth
learns as well as it can to worship the sun
that gives it warmth, sustaining life from day
to day. The complications of the stars
that may affect its fortunes in the woods
are meaningless to it as it waits for dawn.

In a thousand years the notion would never dawn
on it that other forces at work on earth
and heaven may control its life in the woods,
as powerful if more subtle than the sun.
Men recorded the patterns of the stars
and studied what the night implies for the day

as they puzzled out the shapes of their everyday
lives and the structures they make. It was the dawn
of a new idea of ourselves and our place in the stars
that spread as we learned to chart the whirl of the earth
performing its stately dance around the sun,
and light and hope gleamed in the dark woods.

We listened to silence speaking to us in the woods
in apprehension until, on some random day
(or was it random?), along with the bright sun,
there came another, brighter kind of dawn
of knowledge or at least the idea that on earth
we might reach it, aspiring as to the stars

where order flaunts itself and with the stars'
help we grope our way through the present woods
to futurity and the sequences the earth
observes year by year and day by day.
It is always a gift but not a surprise at dawn
when we look to the east and once more see the sun

rise as we knew it would, our mental sun
having already risen. Beyond the stars'
intricacies there are secrets yet to dawn
that may to some degree civilize the woods,
although we cannot imagine that fortunate day
when children may wander safely about the earth.

The other earthly creatures here in the woods
have no such daydreams; they do not reach for the stars
but content themselves at dawn with the rising sun.

Cat's Eyes

If they had souls and if eyes were their windows,
how would we interpret the cat's rapt gaze
of knowingness? Whatever catness knows,
this one has mastered, and nothing else can matter.
Moving things that need therefore to be killed
are fascinating, but her stare has no
evil intent, evil not being a part
of her repertoire, even though the good
or whatever elicits her purr of pure approval
is certain as heaven in saints' imaginations.
That delicate shade of green suggests green thoughts
Marvell taught us to long for. Darkness falls,
but the cat's irises widen and she continues,
as we cannot, rapt and undeterred,
intent on doing whatever it is she does.

Underwood

I watched in incomprehension as her fingers
flew above the keyboard, not like birds
but faster and more precisely—butterflies
in the nerves of which are all they ever need
to escape from predators. My mother's fingers
knew, too, where the letters were for the words
she'd taken down from my father, speech that ascended
into a sky I still see glimpses of

on good days, when a couple of cabbage whites
in the garden over an unimpressive privet
perform an impossible dance that tires my eyes
to look at or my mind to follow, but these
do not tousle my hair or touch my cheek.
But then, as I've come to realize, they don't have to.

The Poem

You are about to read a poem,
but the critic comes, austere, a man of authority,
and offers to help you.
You had not supposed that you needed help,
but his tone of voice and his gold-rimmed spectacles
are evidence of his seriousness.
                                                            Why not?

He picks up the poem, sniffs it,
Holds it to the light this way and that,
then he wads it up, puts it in his mouth, and chews it
slowly, contemplatively, and swallows.

You wait for a while as he digests it
and then excretes it.
He offers you a well-formed, not especially malodorous
turd in a blue and white chamber pot.
"This," he says, "will be better for you."
If you believe him, you are an English major.

Recording Angel

No, of course, you cannot change the past
but neither can you prevent the past from changing.
Sly, shy, it conforms to your mood, says
whatever you want, and is what you want it to be
or fear it might have been, which is not so strange,
because it is not out there but in your mind,
hiding itself away, lurking, waiting
for you to let down your guard so it can pounce

with a list of shameful moments. In better spirits
you find it has cheered up, too, and it gives you glimpses
of moments that weren't so bad. As a reward
or a consolation? Neither. For you see
how few they are, how frail, how long ago,
and how unlikely ever to happen again.

Yankees

My father lay in bed and watched TV,
the Yankees games, although sometimes his eyes
closed, which he explained once was how he'd learned
to follow the team on radio in Bridgeport,
and the play-by-play was as vivid for him as the small
figures on the screen. He was depressed
and now I get it—how the narrow focus
on what the pitcher will do and how the batter
will try to respond to what he deals from the mound
is soothing, blocking out the world's disappointments.
He'd doze off for a while: the games kept going,
but these were from '23 when he was the kid
for whom it mattered how Babe Ruth would do,
or Wally Pipp on first base who, that year,
hit .304, or Lou Gehrig, a rookie
who played only thirteen games. The team went on
to the Series to beat the Giants. (My father ran
to tell his father the news and the old man asked,
"Good for the Yid'n?" shaking his head.) It was
maybe the last good thing, the last good time
my father could remember, a place to float off to.

Revision

"I think occasionally of those who were nearly great"
may also have two adverbs, but at least they're funny
while Spender's are flabby and frankly regrettable.
The line is more interesting, too, because the "truly"
great can be overwhelming or off-putting,
even discouraging, while the "nearly" is something
to work toward or hope for: you are not required
to think about them more than now and then.

They may pop into mind, dropping in
as friends will do impromptu, just passing by.
Such people are a privilege to know
and when you are deep in the dumps you take some comfort
that they seem to like you, will even laugh at your jokes,
and any connection with them is reassuring.

Castaways

What do they know? They're plants, right? They stand there
on their island, which, for them, could be any island.
They hear or more likely feel with their delicate rootlets
what could be surf—they don't recognize tires

on concrete or internal combustion engines.
Still if they're dumb they are not without resources:
plants have patience and are content to wait
years, generations, certain that sooner or later

where they are may turn out to be all right.
Even on traffic islands there can be
that huge jade wave from beyond the horizon
that will bring them the beach they have been waiting for.

All We like Sheep

No sheep would ever say, or, all right, think
"The shepherd is our Lord." They are not good
with metaphors but, stupid as they may be,
they know that the shepherd sooner or later will come
with his curved knife and the sheep always run
whenever they see him. They run from his dog too,
because it bites, but neither one of them means
any good to sheep. On the other hand goats,
forgetting their native caution, come when they're called
and even learn to nibble out of your hand,
denying what's real for these sentimental moments
their herdsman allows them in their foreshortened lives.
The knife waits in its sheath for them too,
so, if they're smarter than sheep, they're also dimmer,
not having learned Abraham's hard lesson.
Matthew's peculiar story about how Jesus
sorts out the sheep and goats assumes that it's hard—
they separate themselves, the believing goats
on one side and the fearful, atheist sheep
all on the other, nervous even there,
to embarrass us, which is why there are no scape-sheep
wandering the wilderness for our sins.

Department of Corrections

Harsh, yes, but it is for their own good,
a refinement of how they see the world, correcting
distortions that are inevitable with lapses
of grammar and syntax. We cannot make them
smarter but we can work to diminish
their disabilities. No longer do we
send them to the galleys, even for grievous
errors that affront God's own creation,

but there is no way for them to be paroled,
the words they'd use not having any fixed meaning,
and their phrases ambiguous, even to themselves.
Each must serve out his complete sentence
until he has learned the letter of the law
and can plead his case without further transgression.

Invention

My father's uncle, I think, or maybe an elder
cousin was an inventor, at least of a method
of asking for money tactfully. The devices
he dreamed up were useful only as pretexts
to save the feelings of those he would put the bite on
as well as his own, which were also no doubt at risk.

You can't just go to a relative (again)
and hold out your hand and beg for money for food.
Avoiding such awkwardness, he offered to sell
shares in his latest scheme or contraption.
                                                            You know
what had to happen: one of the stupid ideas
was for a door that when it was open was closed.

My grandfather laughed and sent him away with nothing
for having abandoned the plausibility
good manners required. But what could he do,
the uncle or cousin, having at last thought up
something that really could work? The revolving door
is, when it's open, closed, and closed when it's open,

as only a poor man can understand,
having seen how God's hand works in the world
and having tried, in all his difficulties,
not to lose his patience or lose faith.

Waiting for Sleep

For half an hour every night, I practice
dying, lying there while my life flashes
by in bits and sharp shards—sins
of speech, sins of silence, sins of action
or inaction—until the surrounding darkness
penetrates and I realize what I have done
that was even worse and managed to repress,
as one must do, in order to keep going.

But these monstrosities lurk and emerge in dreams.
I know they are dreams; what I cannot determine
is whether I am asleep or dead. How
can anyone tell the difference until a gray
dawn arrives that does not bring a pardon
but only a stay for which I ought to be thankful?

Choice

Witold Wandurski said that it all comes down
to the choice between revolution and masturbation.
Nothing else? Mathematics? Drink?
Did Witold get up every morning and decide

again for 2 or B? It's hard to admire,
but blood does not flow in the streets like borscht
and the hopes of the volatile masses are not ignited.
Perhaps later on in the afternoon. Or tomorrow.

Raimon de Roussillon

This *trobador,* this Guillem de Cabestany,
so loved his *domna* as to include in his *vers*
more detail than convention required. One could
without excessive cerebration guess
who the woman was, as Raimon, her husband, did.
The sweet love song in his ears was bitter, harsh,
in other words a *trobar brau,* to which
he wanted to respond in a brutal way
beyond mere versification. He killed
the presumptuous and also indiscreet
Guillem. But that was not yet a work of art.
He cut out the fucker's heart, brought it back to the *castel,*
and directed his cook to do whatever it took
to make it at least palatable or, better,
tasty. (The consequences of failure were dire.)
So a couple of onions, just under a pound of carrots,
and oranges, one squeezed for the juice and the other
cut into small sections. With butter and onions
in eight wedges, he browned in a cocotte
(which is, in one sense, a prostitute, but also
a small baking dish respectable women use)
the heart he'd been given. Then the carrots, white wine,
salt, pepper, the orange juice and the sections,
he cooked for a couple of hours over low heat,
and sprinkled them with chopped cilantro—*voilà,*
prête à servir.

            It was Seremonda's dinner:
she ate it with pleasure, even gusto, and asked
what it was. He told her: Guillem's heart
that he had declared in his well-known poem was hers.
She killed herself that night—not unexpected,
a part of the plan, in fact.
                                    Poetic justice?
Doesn't require words, is better without them.

Salida de Emergencia

I can imagine emergencies in which
there may not be time for a salad: a storm looms up,
flapping the tables' blue canvas umbrellas
or threatening women's hats, and what can one do
but yield to the forces of nature and go inside
to the bar, perhaps for a corretto? But this?
An emergency salad?
                                        Suppose a telephone call
with bad news . . . Might not a salad help?
Tossed greens with a simple vinaigrette
and possibly some of those yellow cherry tomatoes?
It's not such a bad idea, the frivolousness
a compliment to one's equipoise, or a help
in summoning up the self-control that began
as good manners but now, in moments of crisis,
can show itself to be the soul's habit.
Every day, the world comes to an end
and what shall we do unless we have prepared
escarole, radicchio, red leaf lettuce,
and chives with which to nourish our faint spirits?

Conservatory Clerihew

Zoltán Kodály
was a talented gály,
but I'd put my monyi
on Ernst Von Dohnányi.

part two

Renditions

"The Vine and the Billy Goat"

BY LEONIDAS OF TARENTUM

The billy goat gnawed the grape vine down to the roots.
From the ground, what was left of the vine said, "Beast,
sooner or later I shall put forth new shoots,
and grapes, and wine that they will serve at the feast
at which your roasted carcass will lie on a dish.
This is my prophecy, prayer, and ardent wish!"

"Workmen"

ANONYMOUS, FROM THE HEBREW

Like clay in the hands of a potter
who expands it or shrinks it,
so are we in your hands,
God of constant love.

Like a stone in the hands of a mason
who splits it or shatters it,
so are we in your hands,
God of life and death.

Like an axe in the hands of a blacksmith
who heats it or cools it,
so are we in your hands,
God of the poor and oppressed.

Like a helm in the hands of a sailor
who turns it this way or that,
so are we in your hands,
God of kindness and mercy.

Like glass in the hands of a blower
who anneals it or melts it,
so are we in your hands,
pardoner of error and sin.

Like cloth in the hand of a draper
who smoothes it or twists it,
so are we in your hands,
O God of vengeance.

Like silver in the hands of a smith
who alloys or refines it,
so are we in your hands,
healer of wounds.

"Red Lips"

ANONYMOUS, GREEK FOLK SONG

Her lips were so red . . .
                                        All right, how red?
I kissed them and mine immediately were red.
I wiped my lips: my handkerchief was red.
I washed it in the river: the river was red,
and the shore was red, and then the sea was red.
An eagle drank from its water: his wings were red.
And then, as he flew, the sun and the moon turned red.

"Lament for Bion"

ANONYMOUS, FROM THE GREEK, C. 100 BCE

Weep, you Sicilian muses, in sweet pity:
the mallow dies in the garden, the parsley and dill
also die, but then, in the following year
spring up again.
                                        It is not so with us.
Strong men, wise, great, and powerful, die.
From our endless sleep in the earth there is no waking.

"Provençal Poets"

BY DENIS OF PORTUGAL

The Provençeaux are able to write fine verse,
and they say that it's love that fills them with inspiration,
but they who can only address themselves to creation
in the season when flowers bloom . . . What do they know?
They're lightweights; their hearts are never filled with woe,
as mine is. I write better when I feel worse.

They toss off clever and finely embellished lays
about their ladies all of whom are fine,
and we can agree that women and roses and wine
are agreeable and you'd have to be dense indeed
not to enjoy them. Their poems are fun to read,
but God knows a man's heart can break some days.

Those who only celebrate and praise
the pretty flowers of springtime, where do they go
when that happy season passes and there are no
twittering birds to rhyme about? Uninspired
without Joy's fleeting muses, they
soon grow tired;
my grief is loyal and faithful and it stays.

"Of the Deceitful Brevity of Life"

BY LUIS DE GONGORA

The arrow's flight to the bull's-eye is not so fast;
the chariot on the track near the grandstand
makes even less sound as its wheels in the sand
spin in a silent blur when it hurtles past

than our age which rushes onward at such a rate
that takes away the breath. The sun in the sky
is a speeding comet, whatever the naked eye
reports or however we ratiocinate.

Carthage bears witness to this, as who can deny?
It is at your peril, Licio, then, that you fly
after ephemeral shadows that dart and play.

The hours are all too brief as they scurry by,
grinding down the days, as you and I
see how days can nibble the years away.

"Give Way to God, or The Dying Christ"

BY PIERRE DE FERMAT

to Jean-Louis Guez de Balzac

Intelligence, deluded, often stood there stunned,
preferring a foolish play of colors to true lights.
Poor Reason, what wars do you wage, what overthrown
antique deities do you call upon obliquely
with elegant twists and tropes of your far-too-clever tongue?
Have those old notions, so long dormant now, revived
the pagan gods to the awe they used to inspire in men?
Hiding away, locked in Pluto's dismal kingdom
or in the Elysian Fields, do they still wield the power
to will belief on our part? Press on, nevertheless,
along those paths where Balzac has already shown the way.
Do not be distracted or interrupt your progress
to dawdle among the silent oaks of Dodona's grove
or attend to words they claim come from the mute Phoebus,
but yield to God. Descendants of ancient heaven-dwellers
have given way already and in unison they declare,
"God! Behold God!" Nature, bowing low,
acknowledges him as her parent. To him the earth, the seas,
and the blasts of storms in the air are tame and loving subjects.
For him do the very clouds moderate their voices,
the control of which is no longer their own. His dazzling light
shines with a pure brightness, for he pulled light out of light,
the one God whose eternal mind from his birth onward
exuded eternity. The Supreme Father, he took
the garments of mortal flesh to bend the hearts of men
to a new course and wring out the last droplets of love
from grudging human spirits. It was no easy labor,
for the Parent handed over the Son's scourged body
to wretchedness and madness, such that he in heaven
groaned aloud too and contorted his notional limbs
in an agony they had never experienced before.

As if he had not yet cleansed the world of its many sins
and as if this appalling torment were not at all excessive,
he said, "Behold, here I am, the sacrificial lamb;
willingly I submit myself to the pain of death.
Consider, then, the body, dripping with blood and sweat.
Even if you reject the entire idea of salvation,
look into the eyes of a man who suffers unfairly."
Thus he spoke as he raised his face to the distant stars.
What prayers did he then pour out? What pitiable sighs
broke from his burdened body, doing his father's bidding
and, at the same time, preparing himself for the further
strenuous labors that would be required of mind and will?
Meanwhile, descending from heaven was the comfort for which he had prayed,
and there it was—the noise of the threatening mob receded
and in its place was support from the heavenly powers watching
the punishment who came to surround the waiting cross.
He said, then: "Supreme Being, why do you thus delay?
Why do you intercede now to postpone these dangers
for which I have prepared? Why do you interfere
with obstacles in the path of my not-yet-fulfilled love?"
Having said that, he feels his flesh once again succumb
to its mortal condition and mind, to trouble and human doubt.
His gait is no longer steady. In this condition, he spends
the night in prayer. His companions, who ought to keep watch with him,
are sound asleep, unaware of his impending trial
and the prayers he offers. The business of heaven is far beyond them
Where is their honor? Their courage? Of what effect are their oaths
of loyalty to their teacher's commands? None of these matter.
He wanders alone and hears a rumbling all around him
from the shadowy pines on which a hostile power impinges.
It is under the weight of that very wood that he fails at last,
suffering lashes and thorns, and then affixed to the cross,
driven on by his love and desire for our salvation
that assuages the dreadful torments his torn limbs undergo.
He knows that death is approaching, the destiny of mortals,
and he trembles while the mad crowd, now turning against him,
hurl their jeers and insults. For these degenerate people

he prays for life and peace. Never once does he wish
for his torturers the pains that they are inflicting on him.
And then, after a long time, it is over, his bloody
body streaked with purple that flowed from its many wounds.
It is not an easy passage. His mind is not at peace,
for he strains upwards and calls in a resonant voice, "Father,
why do you abandon me now that death approaches?
Why do you torment me with your own and your people's rage?
We have given you and the world more than enough, for now
every prophecy has been fulfilled in every detail."
Dying, his luminous aura resorbs into the earth
and his powers to see into Heaven fade away. His soul
dims and his body's husk calls out with its last breath,
"I commend this soul to you, exalted parent." And then . . .
he stirred no more, having departed life on earth.
So, sometimes, you see in a lamp, through its vent hole,
as it gutters out it produces a momentary brightness
with energy from somewhere but then it fades again
to the blackness of soot. In him there was that same spark
that glowed bright for an instant and then was carried away
despite whatever wan resistance it could muster
to be stored away forever in the shadows of endless night.
But no, not even eternal night can extinguish the light
you will bring for the third time—the birth, the resurrection,
and then the third and final coming we all await
when the earth and the souls of men will be revived and renewed.
Meanwhile, you lead me onward and upward, Balzac: my Muse
helps me traverse the high passes that you have explored.
She labors on without you, doing the best she can
with my own paltry work. I entertain modest hopes
of ascending Pierian heights with work that may stand with yours
and that you will be kind to it for it is your progeny too,
created as it has been in order to do you honor.

"The Battle of Maldon"

ANONYMOUS, FROM THE OLD ENGLISH

. . . was broken.
He had each man abandon his horse
driving it far so he could march
forward unfettered his mind on his hands
and the blade of his sword with its edge of honor.
Great Offa's kinsman when he first understood
the earl would not now tolerate cowards
set free from his hand his favorite hawk
to fly high on the wind away to the forest.
Forging them forward shoreward, warward,
that lusty lad would not shrink from the moment
as any man might see for himself
when it was time to hold his weapon.
Eadric likewise, eager to serve
his lord in the combat, carried his spear,
daring, determined with sword hand and shield hand
to vindicate vows given the master.
Byrhtnoth then began to arrange in order
his muster of men in the best dispositions,
how they should hold homestead ground
their round-shields aligned together in good grip
and with broadswords ready and not be frightened.
When they were rightly arrayed as he wanted
he dismounted at last to stand on the turf
hard by his hearth's men closest and most loyal.

The Viking herald, strident, shouting
from shore declared the Vikings' clear purpose.
His errand: to tell the earl the terms
of the seafarers' message from the ships on the bank:
"Send in all speed to the valiant seamen
treasure to take. Buy your safety,
paying them tribute to avoid battle.

We see no need for wanton destruction
for you are wealthy and we can deal—
for gold to give the advantage of truce.
If you and your council consider our offer
you will send us seafarers away from Essex
and redeem your people with the peace all men want.
We will go willingly, your gold in our coffers,
traveling elsewhere and leave you alone."
Byrhtnoth spoke hefting his shield
and ashen spear, to answer for all:
"Hear them, seaman? Hark at my host.
What they will pay is spears they will send
with poisoned points and their family swords,
those heriot weapons not for your profit.
Go then, envoy, say to your seamen
our terse terms— that the English earl
stands fast with his troops, defends his homeland,
and defies your demands upon Aethelred's realm,
his land and his people. In hard battle
heathens will fall, for it would be shameful
that you should depart in your plundering ships
without the fight that we must give you.
Thus far have you come into our country,
but fare no farther or think to extort
what is ours from us. Point and sharp edge
must carve the conclusion, who gives and who takes,
and settle the terms before we pay tribute.

He bade them then to heft their shields
and all advance to the bank of the river
where water would ward one troop from the other
while the flood tide took its own time turning.
They waited for water, the Pante's current,
where waterstreams locked to ebb and allow
the spearmen to move and, patient, watched
the ship-army of Viking invaders.
Both sides were harmless except for arrows'

feathered flight   till the tide moved out,
and the many Vikings in ranks   eager for war
stood in massed menace.   Byrhtnoth then ordered
Wulfstan, Ceola's son,   his hero to guard the bridge
the bravest of brethren.   When the first of the Danes
approached the bridge,   with sharp spear-shot
he cut him down.   Alongside Wulfstan,
stood Aelfhere and Maccus,   a fine pair of steadfast men
who would not deign   to flee from that ford
but defied the foe   with the weapons they wielded.
When the Vikings discovered   these gallant bridge-guards
they fell back, dissembling,   and craved, as if craven,
permission to put ashore   to lead their men safely
into battle and blood-risk.   The earl, overconfident,
granted them passage,   too much land
to those hateful people,   and Byrhthelm's son, Byrhtnoth,
called across the chill water   as his host harkened:
"The pathway is open.   Come to us quickly,
war-men meeting war-men.   God alone knows
who will win control   of this killing field."

Advancing then, the Viking army,   careless of water,
crossed the Pant westward,   lifting high
their linden shields.   Opposed, the fierce
forces of Byrhtnoth   then formed a war-wall,
shield next to shield,   to hold off the attack,
for the crisis had come,   the time of trial
where the men who are fated   will fall as they must.
Overhead ravens   and carrion-hungry
screeching eagles   made leisurely circles,
while below the massed men   sent their roar skyward,
followed by sharp-filed   spears they flung.
Bows, too, were busy,   and Viking shields
bristled with arrows.   The war-charge then
was fierce, and men fell   leaving the ground
a clutter of corpses,   and Wulfmar wounded
and sliding to death-rest   he could not refuse.

Byrhtnoth's kinsman, his sister's son,
was hard-hacked by many swords.
But the wound was redressed as Edward offered
payment in kind, and a doomed fighter,
as I have heard, fell at his feet.
For this his lord thanked him at the earliest moment,
telling his chamberlain. Thus, they stood,
firm and strong-minded, men in hard battle,
keen in competing whose pointed weapons might
find their way to fated men
and garner the lives of those men of war.
Dying men fell but the steadfast and resolute
still stood as Byrhtnoth gave his heartening words,
that whoever strove now to achieve great glory
should look to the Danes to drag it from them.

The bold one, Byrhtnoth, raised up his weapon
and set his shield to stride toward a soldier,
the earl to the churl and each meaning evil.
That seaman marauder hurled his southern spear
and wounded was the warriors' lord.
Byrhtnoth banged the shaft, shaking it free
and stabbed with the spear-point its Viking owner,
giving him back the bite of its wound.
Skillful was Byrhtnoth and he struck with his lance,
hitting the Viking and piercing his neck
and in that quick thrust reaching his life.
He turned to another and hurled at this Viking
that lance that landed and pierced through his chainmail
the hard point hitting his heart.
Elated, the earl, the valiant victor,
laughed aloud and gave thanks to his God
for the work of the day, the deity's grant.
But one Viking then loosed from his hand
a javelin, striking Aethelred's noble thane,
Byrhtnoth, and biting into his body.
Hard by his side a fledgling fighter,

Wulfstane's son the young Wulfmaer
drew from his lord the bloodied spear
and flung it forward back at that Viking
to get him for getting the lad's lord.
This strike was successful and the Viking lay dying.
Came then another Viking marauder
up to the earl to harvest rich pickings,
rings and armor and patterned sword.
But Byrhtnoth could draw his blade from its scabbard
to strike at that sailor and would have, but one
of the cut-throat's comrades hit the earl's arm
and rendered it useless. His biting blade then
fell to the earth, for Byrhtnoth could no more
hold the weapon's weight. Still, he could speak,
that white-haired war man, to encourage his people
and urge them onward. His legs were unsteady
and footing uncertain, as the hero to heaven
spoke his last words: "I give you my thanks,
O King of Kings, for all my achievements
in this life I have lived. Now, my king Maker,
I ask a last favor, that you may admit me
into your high domain. Lord of the Angels,
grant peaceful passage and hear my petition
that the demons of hell not snare my spirit."
Then heathen men hacked him and his two companions,
Aelfnoth and Wulfmaer who had stood beside him
and, along with their lord, they too gave their lives.

They then fled the battle whose spirit for the fighting
began now to quaver: Odda's son, Godric,
was the first man who fled, abandoning Byrhtnoth
who had given him many mares and their trappings and tack.
He leapt on his lord's own charger
who had not ever earned the right to ride and use,
and he and his brothers, Godwine and Godwig,
flew from the battle they could not bear,
away from the fighting to hide in the forest.

to find there some refuge   and save their hides,
they and many more   spiritless men
who each had received   Byrhtnoth's favors.
Offa had warned him   early that day
at the morning meeting   in the counsel-place
that many who spoke   the speeches of warriors
might not at need   be worth their fine words.

Æthelred's earl,   their leader, lay dead,
and all who saw   Byrhtnoth's body,
the proud thanes   and the household troops,
brave men now   hastened keenly,
seeing but two   choices of honor:
either to die there   along with their lord,
or else to avenge him,   and kill many Danes.
Ælfwin, Ælfric's young son,   urged them all onward
making his valorous speech: "Remember those times
after much mead   there in the great hall
we were such heroes   making proud vows
of our bearing in battle,   the times of tough fighting.
Now we discover   which ones are brave.
I pray that my progeny   declare with some pride
among Mercian men   of noble line
that I was here.   My grandfather, Ealhelm,
an earl of much wisdom,   did well in the world.
Let no one now taunt me   that I wanted to go
away from this army   home and to safety
when my leader lay   cut down in the fighting,
my kinsman, my lord,   the greatest of griefs."
Then he moved forward   hot with his hatred
and with his weapon-point   found one of the Vikings
impaling the pirate   to leave him lying
dead on the ground.   With this he could rally
as much as his words did   his friends and his comrades
to advance toward the enemy.   Offa spoke up
shaking his ash-spear: "Yea, Ælwin has said it
to urge you all on,   the good thanes at need-time.

Byrhtnoth lies dead, our earl on the earth,
and this is our moment to rally each other
forward to war, holding our hard blades
of spear and sharp sword. The coward, Godric,
Odda's get, has betrayed us, fleeing the field
on Byrhtnoth's own mount, thus dispersing the army
and breaking the shield-wall. Damn him for what he did,
spreading his foul fear among the formation!"
Leofsun then spoke, raising his linden shield:
"I offer my oath. Not one step backward!
I fare only forward to avenge in hard battle
my good lord's death. The brave men of my village,
the people of Sturmer, will not have the need
to reproach my behavior. My friend has fallen
and I am lordless. I will not go home
or turn away from the fight, but a weapon must take me,
point or sharp blade edge." He advanced in his anger
and steadfast he fought, scorning the flight.
Dunner spoke up as he brandished his weapon.
An honest peasant, he called out to all,
bidding each soldier to avenge great Byrhtnoth:
"Let no one hesitate who intends to wreak vengeance
on the Viking horde, nor fear for his life!"
And then they moved forward, indifferent to death.

Into the fight, then, the brave spear-bearers
advanced to avenge their stricken good lord,
and prayed to the Lord that they might destroy Danes.
Their hostage helped them, a Northumbrian captive,
Edglaf's son, Ashfroth, of hardy kin.
He joined in the struggle, firing arrows.
Some stuck in shields but some pierced Vikings,
and on and on he fought, wielding his weapon
as long as he could. The tall Edward,
fierce in the front line, shouted defiance
and said he would never yield one foot of land
when his lord lay dead. He broke through their shield wall

and with fellow fighters collecting from Vikings
blood for Byrhtnoth's blood. Æthric, also,
a noble warrior, pressing forward
wreaked worthy vengeance. He, Sibricht's brother,
and many more with him split the Danes' targes
and defended themselves as chain-mail sang
its shrill terror-songs. Offa in battle
struck one of the seamen who fell to the turf:
Gad's kinsman fell, cut down in the fighting.
Still, he had fulfilled his oath to his lord,
the ring-giver Byrhtnoth, that they return together
into the town or else die together
from wounds on the slaughter-field. Noble, he lay there
close to his lord. Then were shields crashing
as the Vikings, enraged, fought their way forward,
their sharp spears piercing life-boxes.
Wystan advanced, Thurstan's son,
and hot in the hurly-burly felled three of their fighters
before he himself lay dead on the ground.
There was hard fighting with warriors standing firm
in the hard struggle. Worn down by wounds
fighters fell. All the while,
Oswold and Eadwold, two brawny brothers,
exhorted the men, their cousins and kinsmen,
to stand firm and to use their good weapons.
Then Byrhtwold spoke up, raising his shield,
an older fighter, shaking his ash-spear
and exhorting the men: "Your minds put in order,
and settle your hearts. Our courage must grow
as the strength we have ebbs. Here lies our leader,
a good man in the dirt. Any who leave now
will ever be sorry for quitting this war work
to survive then in shame. I have lived long
and I know much of life, but I shall not leave here.
My firm intention is here to be killed
to lie by the side of the lord I have loved."
Godric, too, Ethelgar's son,

called them to battle,   and hurling his javelin,
a death-spear flying   into the Vikings.
And he with his friends   advanced on the Danes,
hacking at them   and cutting them down
until he, himself,   was killed in the combat—
a far different Godric   than he who had run . . .

www.ingramcontent.com/pod-product-compliance
Lightning Source LLC
LaVergne TN
LVHW050941080826
845145LV00004B/1357

* 9 7 8 0 8 0 7 1 5 1 8 0 8 *